Nora Gomringer is one of Germ; contemporary poets. In the early voice in Germany's young slam s(performance continues to inform the boundaries between performa as often intersecting with other art forms, from film to music and visual art. She's won a number of awards for her writing, from the Jacob Grimm German Language Prize in 2011 to the prestigious Ingeborg Bachmann Award in 2015.

Annie Rutherford makes things with words, and champions poetry and translated literature in all its guises. She has divided her working life between Germany and Scotland, and is now programme co-ordinator for StAnza, Scotland's international poetry festival, as well as a freelance translator. She co-founded Göttingen's Poetree festival, edited the literary magazine *Far Off Places* and makes comics with illustrator Beth Barnett.

Hydra's Heads

Nora Gomringer

Translated by Annie Rutherford

Ricky,
Ich werde
etwas mit der Sprache
machen...

Annie †

Burning Eye

The translation of this work was supported by a grant from the Goethe-Institut which is funded by the German Ministry of Foreign Affairs.

The poems in the book are English translations of poems from the following books:

achduje © Nora Gomringer und Der gesunde Menschenversand Luzern, 2015

Mein Gedicht fragt nicht lange © Nora Gomringer und Verlag Voland & Quist, 2011

Mein Gedicht fragt nicht lange reloaded © Nora Gomringer und Verlag Voland & Quist, 2015

This is for Friederike Mayröcker was originally published in *Poem: International Quarterly* 6(2), summer 2018.

This edition published by Burning Eye Books 2018

www.burningeye.co.uk

@burningeyebooks

Burning Eye Books
15 West Hill, Portishead, BS20 6LG

ISBN 978-1-911570-44-8

Printed & bound by ImprintDigital.com, UK

BurningEyeBooks
Never Knowingly
Mainstream

Hydra's Heads

CONTENTS

Poems credited as from:
Silbentrennung,
Sag doch mal was zur Nacht,
Klimaforschung,
and
Nachrichten aus der Luft
are from the book
Mein Gedicht fragt nicht lange reloaded

Poems credited as from:
Gedichte
are from the book
Mein Gedicht fragt nicht lange

Poems credited as from:
achduje
are from the book
achduje

I'M GOING TO DO SOMETHING WITH LANGUAGE

For J. H.

I'm now going to do something with language
I'll now do something quite particular, peculiar with language
You'll be astonished
I'll do something quite astonishing with language
You'll want to clutch at your partner's hand, it'll be so utterly
Astonishing
Even if you don't want to be astonished because you know it
     all and you've seen it all and so on
It'll still be quite astonishing and unexpected, even
     unforeseeable
You'll maybe want to call God or your parents
It'll be that astonishing, what I now intend to do with language
It'll be quite unheard of, what I'll do now with language, this
     something
It'll seem astonishing to you, almost incomprehensible to your
     senses
This language, my language, its effect
What it will spark
I'll show you something with your language
Will wrest something from this language you know by heart
You'll be astonished, you will be
By how I wrestle with it
What I am doing with your language
Will be so incomprehensible to you
That you'll glance at your neighbour, amazed and quite out of
     breath
I shall do something quite extraordinary with this language
     you know so well
This language you use
I'll do this
Soon
You just have to stick with me, as I now
Yes, you could say, conjure, maybe you'd like to say
That I'm conjuring, am working something like magic

Now with your damn language
Which you like, you own, is yours
Yeah, yeah, no worries, it's yours
I will conjure beautiful birds or stars from it
By caesarean section
I will do nothing with your language
If you don't keep listening and pay attention
Watch, why don't you, as I do something extraordinary with
    language
Just watch how I do it, how I could do it, what I could do if
    you'd only bloody let me
So much could be done with language, so much which is just
    unbelievable
Phenomenal and remarkably powerful if you'd just let me
Why won't you let me
Well, this'll clearly come to nothing
Nothing extraordinary or astonishing with language
This'll come to
Absolutely zilch, such a shame, without any magic at all,
    nothing will happen with language
If you don't pay attention to this incredible language, this
    quite extraordinary, familiar, oh-so-familiar language so
    changed by my work, then this will turn to something
    quite different, far removed from the original idea, this will
    all turn to
Nothing

From *Klimaforschung*

I NEVER TOLD YOU

I never told you how I came by my name.

I licked it up, carried it away from the walls. I stretched it out on a screen to dry, illuminated and magnified.

At first nobody wanted to hear it. All of them were bitter at my taking liberties.

I stole my name for myself from public squares and in return sprayed the words of the prophet on the subway walls.

I kissed it off strange lips and the dark muzzles of dogs.

Scraped it up off park benches, watched as it boarded the train for Rome.

On coloured paper I copied it a hundred times to hang in the display cases and window panes of butchers and florists.

I licked its lie from my parents' fingers and trickled it into small bottles at the back of sock drawers.

As though it were wax, I melted it and let it run into my ears until I was deaf.

This is how I came by my name. Just like this. But not only.

From *Gedichte*

WITH THE LIGHT

With the light
that falls on your shoes
and that you kick further away
with every step
the darkness too loses ground,
slips past your brisk
brilliant steps
into the last corners.
Underneath the streetlight
you look
like a large moth
and I don't trust myself
to watch any longer
for perhaps your wings
have dried already.

From *Gedichte*

SPIDERS

The notes fall onto my thighs like fine dust
for I am sitting near the stage.
The movements, the largos, the allegros are falling into my lap
and want to crawl inside me.
I listen closely to the small hammers and strings
in the grand dark body
so that all the images imprint themselves yet more clearly
upon me.
The pianist's fingers
which run down the keys like spiders
and weave and spin the white and black
into their cocoon of chords.
It all flutters down around me
and onto me and into me,
and the tones slowly gather the skirts and shirts
they'd only just taken off to play at love
and get dressed in shame
without another look at me,
without making another sound.
We go our separate ways.
I stand up to applaud.
The dust falls from my lap onto my feet
and so it is easy to carry it outside.
The tones have faded away, and the violent love has too.
The pianist has taken his hands from the keys.
I don't look back. I take one step at a time,
the notes softly swinging.

From *Gedichte*

SPEECHLESS AND SPARE

one by one
I pack my hairs
the brown and the fair
into the suitcase standing ready
in the hall
where the light always fell on your mouth
and our farewells
smelt best
syllable for syllable
I swallow
the dried words
back inside me
without tasting their weight
this time
or licking their vowels

and sustained by this stale dish
I can set out
for I have become spare
and speechless

From *Gedichte*

SHE HOLDS HER LASHES

she holds her eyelashes
between the pinch of the tweezers

she frees them all from the union
of the dark frame

she endures each short pain
and the tear that follows

she observes her lashless
eyes like stagnant ponds

she makes a wish on each hair
from her lids for a small pinch of luck

she knows: that's not how it works

From *Gedichte*

THE WAY YOU WILL NOT LEAVE

the way you will not leave
my mind
long after you
have left the minds
of everybody else
this way I'll pass your
laughter on to my
unborn children
this way I gift your
touch to my
next beloved
this way I let you
determine how my
kisses continue to taste

and I can say
that I bear it

for there is no grave here
only a place in me
where I shall let you
lead a long life
until you give me to understand
that I will be
fully
without you
if that is what I want

From *Gedichte*

SOMETIMES

sometimes
the soul is
that thing
which the cat
after hunting
drags home
no more
than a
dead mouse
and yet
you still
jump
onto the chair
in flight

From *Gedichte*

MATHEMATICAL FANTASY

beneath the angle
between their legs
sine and cosine dance
intersecting
closely

From *Gedichte*

INSTRUCTIONS

So
Now
Then
Always
Just
So

From *Silbentrennung*

UNSAID

Clench
Your jaws tight together
Erode
The mountain range of words
Swallow
The resultant sand

Raise up the words
Inside to dunes

From *Silbentrennung*

VARIATION ON A THEME

On parting
Rip off your lips

Disroot your teeth
Torch the fields
Of your tongue's tastebuds

Bite firmly into the flesh
Inside your cheek

Talk the uvula
Out of remembering

From *Silbentrennung*

DISCOVERING DIALECT

someone collects the heard
and spoken words
holds them with pins
against white fabric
in a case of glass
dyes his skin
with coloured words
faces the speaker in silence
to catch the language
untainted

From *Silbentrennung*

VERBAL DIALYSIS

on your tongue
digesting the word

allowing the split
reshaping it
with enzymes

to become
indecipherable
and travelling through

the bloodstream
in U-turns
causing the components

to clot
shifted with sweetness
and transporting

to the kidneys
the alphabet
with the omega

From *Silbentrennung*

LAST ORDERS

out of the noise at night
a planet
gives birth to itself
on a silent orbit
the centre of which
is you
to which you rise
from the depths beneath
the stones of the street
whispering delirium drenched
in smoke and music
join others
going into
the next place
which will strip you bare
there where
the night
spits you from its stomach
underneath the pole star

From *Silbentrennung*

ESKIMO FOLK TALE

the sun hot with shame
the brother in her bed
so in love with her

she readied the carriage
and to escape him travelled
along the sky

the brotherly moon
cannot find her
blinded

From *Silbentrennung*

FLATLINING

Positioned like this
The pulse serves
As a compass
For the trek

From dust to lust
All with a long story
You can reveal

Or eloquently conceal
And through
The binding of the Hippocratic oath
Only offstage for
Three last beats

From *Silbentrennung*

EARTHQUAKE ATMOSPHERE

this way I am
your seismograph

catch your trembling
in my nerves

use it to build myself
a house and live there

for too long

From *Silbentrennung*

SUPPOSITION

you tell me
of the clouds dashing
through the sky
after work's done

how they
overtook you
in your head
between your thoughts

the storm forced
them into place
by the shop
as if in fast forward

did you maybe
ask yourself where
this would lead

From *Silbentrennung*

WINTER RETROSPECTIVE

how readily
everything which had
to do with summer
spells itself
summer vocabulary
fills our mouths
till we could spit fire
even words
for the lizard
plucked from the crack
reptilian tail
scorched in the sun

From *Silbentrennung*

OBSERVATION

the way the rain clings
onto the treetops
swinging his
waterfeet
till they brush against
the coat shoulders
of passers by

all reflected
pictures from behind
around on their
own axis and
back again
shattering the threads
in all water

passing by
the steps get
quicker

From *Silbentrennung*

THE THING ABOUT POETRY

Peanuts.
A phone call at 2.30am: wwhat? Whasswrong?
Sometimes a party and a crisis.
A question: how come you can, just not in Berlin?
Writing and doing this (*scrunching up paper*) and this
    (*chucking it over your shoulder*).
And still always writing.
And then…
Nothing. Black.
Void. Depression. Doctor's appointment. Sensing lumps.
Decent medicines.
Then, can, could, would you read this sometime and let me
    know what you think?
Soul searching, researching, word counting.
Not installed. Not installed.
Not poetic.
Colleagues: yeah, but somehow it's all been done before. The
    hormones need to get off the stage.
An apology.
A duty and a pleasure.
Stuff strutting, book buying, exhaling, absconding, exploding.
                                        Unwinding.

And then a compliment.
A publication, a kick up the arse.
A comparison too,
Interviews with Charlotte. What the higgins?
And a business-class queue for business-class seats,
A language at last, at some point. A theme,
A publication date and a neighbour at the fence.
Maybe a postcard: your book in my hand, here by the sand.
The thing about poetry:
Rolling cigarettes,
Ogling the girls,
Lolling at the corner,
Rock 'n' rolling rhymes.
The thing about poetry:
Poetic? Hardly.

From *Sag doch mal was zur Nacht*

HOLOFERNES, 3RD FLOOR

It's around seven. Although I don't really do much, I normally never make it home before seven o'clock. By then everyone else is already sitting in the kitchen, eating dinner. Mia, Joris, the lesbian couple, and often friends of the lesbians as well. I walk past the kitchen to my room. It looks the way it did this morning. I left the window open, so it's a little colder. I take your head out of my shoulder bag. It has oozed quite a bit. I hadn't really thought about the blood. Your face is no longer beautiful. I am disappointed. As if I had ordered something from a catalogue which doesn't live up to its picture. I cut a plastic bag open at the sides and spread it out on the desk. There. You fit well on there. I have to turn you away a bit because you are very pale and your eyes have rolled horribly. I have to admit, I'm disappointed.

When Mia knocks, I just call 'yes!' and when she enters, I apologise for the temperature of the room and the blood on the carpet. Mia says that she just wanted to say 'hello' quickly and to ask if I'd be joining them in the kitchen. 'Hello, Mia,' I say and smile at her. I turn on the TV. On the news they say that you are missed and that police dogs are being deployed to search for your head. Mia simply says, 'But it's here,' and we both smile. I decide on the kitchen and leave your head here. In the kitchen, Joris offers us a slice of his pizza. I don't say no. Judith never says no.

From *Sag doch mal was zur Nacht*

MY DOG AND THE TORAH

שמע ישראל אדוני אלוהינו אדוני אחד. Hear, dearly beloved, how I am the master, your only master. Who had to let you go. Who chose the day on which a car, a person to accompany me, a quick lunch would be available, a doctor could be reached. A day on which the sun would rain and the rain would shine, a day on which it wouldn't matter on which side anyone got out of bed. A day. A day following on from a night, a day. Simply a day. A day with as many hours as the sum of two times twelve. A day with a middle, a caesura, several curtains, scene changes, smoke and mirrors, a day, a gathering of objects, a collection of curiosities, a day, a domain of seconds, a day.

The way you lay on the table. And the way I said yeeees in a Moses cry and the doctor parted the tides of the sea for me and filled a syringe and I thought no and wept no and meant no and was no and no and no. On the day which was to be your last and my last with you and my first without you and my day and soon no longer yours and mine and yours and I was a thief who took your days from you and the doctor was a thief who took you from me.

Dad drove with Mum and the spade in the boot to the tree. You lay wrapped in blankets like baby Jesus, so heavy without sighs, without days because I had let all your days be stolen. Dad dug and dug and destroyed the roots of the linden tree and made the tree sway under which you should have lain and would have lain and should have wanted to lie and Mum carried you carefully, like a feather, a pillow made of feathers, a world made of feathers, a small sun of feathers, a small moon of feathers and ash and stone to the grave into which you were lowered, enwrapped in your French dress, your red and black stripes. Here you are to rest, while we bleach the places on the sofa, under the counter in the kitchen, the rug by the radiator, the patch of sunlight on the straw mat under the window, so that they are always yours and you recognise them when you return. On the day of the Last Judgement, right behind the dog of the Messiah, for I am sure that he had one.

From Sag doch mal was zur Nacht

THE GROUND FLOOR

Hello.
I would like to show you around.
Show you everything.
I would like to show you around and show you everything.
I'm not rude.
I'm not rude.
I am trying not to be rude.
I'm very tired.
But not rude. I wouldn't want to be thought of as rude.
When you are visiting me.
Are actually visiting me.
When someone is actually visiting me again.
I don't want to come across as rude.
I have tidied and hoovered, first of all I swept, dampened the
    cloths, wiped the furniture down slowly with the damp
    cloths, without gloves on, took the pictures and their
    frames from the piano, wiped them too with damp cloths,
    put them back in their places, picked up the newspapers,
    folded them or chucked them straight out, I decrumbed
    the toaster, cleaned the oven, thawed out and cleaned the
    fridge, cleaned the toilets, cleaned the bath, decalced the
    showerhead, I thought about the garden.
About planting.
About putting in new plants.
I thought about the pots in the cupboards, about the broom
    handles, the sponges in the sink, the nail brushes. About
    all the last little bits of soap.
I would like to show you around, but not on the second floor.
Don't ask me about the first floor. I would like to show you
    around.
Don't ask me about the first floor.
I am trying not to be rude. Trying not to think beyond the
    ground floor while doing so.
There is no first floor in my house, not really. Therefore no
    second floor either.
No heavens above it.
So don't ask me about them.

I have tidied.
Have after two months found order.
Tidied down here.
The ground floor clings to the earth.
There is none above it.
No one would speak of heaven if the ground floor would suffice.
I've prepared a bite to eat.
It's very sweet. The children like it very sweet.

Liked.
No walls, no rooms, no beds, no last bits of soap by the sink,
    no footsteps from the first floor.
No footsteps from the first floor.
Eight weeks ago I stood in a hospital.
Heard what a doctor said, was hugged by a sister and thought
    I was crying.
For eight weeks there has been no first floor in my house.
My bedroom, my bathroom, the children's beds disappeared
    with my husband and daughters.
Now I am being rude.
I had been trying not to be rude.
I wanted to try not to be rude.
You shouldn't have asked about the first floor.
No footsteps from the first floor.
The ground floor clings to the earth.

From *Sag doch mal was zur Nacht*

ASSUMPTIONS ABOUT THE TOWN

In the town live people.
In the town live dogs.
However. More people than dogs.
Presumably. Who knows?
In the town beat hearts.
There's quite a nightlife.
It's all downhill from here,
Then left at the back, say the rats.
In the different parts of town you see the whole.
Kerfuffle.
Sometimes the wrong people go off the rails. Or fall onto them.
The streets are paved with gold. Here, and elsewhere.
Friends of your parents live in the town. They say, pay us a call
    sometime.
They've known you since you were so small.
(*Their gesture while saying this is ridiculous. You were never
    that small.*)
Fathers and mothers split up in this town and fathers take their
    lovers to fancy restaurants because that's what lovers like.
    Meanwhile, mothers cut the heads of fathers out of photo
    albums. Children watch these goings-on and decide not to
    ever get married.
People live in this town without knowing anyone else. Everyone
    looks like Adam.
In this town people are waiting for Jesus.
In this town people are waiting for buses.
And for the train. Always for the train.
In this town lives someone who looks like someone I know.
Wordsworth came through this town once.
Wordsworth said it wasn't worth it.
In this town some sleep while others are watchful.
In this town everyone has someone they are close to.
You are closest to me. In this town.
Pulses beat in this town. And the far right is beating up lefties.
And lamps sway on cables diagonally across the streets.
In this town they built on sand.
Here they dug down deep and found themselves.

In this town they stood and watched. The trains leaving with
the Jews.
The long legs of the pretty girls in the short skirts.
In this town women talk in a different way with women than
men do with women.
Here letterboxes are not places of sin.
You returned here after all those years and no one recognised
you. You might as well have stayed away.
This is a place people leave.
In this town there are streets which lead back to themselves.
Here there are people who climb up ladders to gaze at
shooting stars.

From *Sag doch mal was zur Nacht*

MONOLOGUE

I have sewn diamonds into the hem of your skirt
    so that you can buy bread
I have put your teddy in the rucksack
    and a jar of jam as well, but shhh
I have rolled your slips into the sheets
    you must unpack them quickly
I have stuffed the papers right to the bottom
    of this pocket, so that no one, you know
I have stitched a little money into the coat
    perhaps you can
I have Grandfather's watch in the vase by the window
    they shouldn't stop you
I have put a pen in this envelope and with it
    a letter to your uncle, give it to him
I have removed the star from your jacket
    it's better that way
I have burnt all the stars
    now every night is black
It seems I have given all my advice
    now I have none left
I have sewn diamonds into the hem of your skirt
    but shhh

From *Sag doch mal was zur Nacht*

AND IT WAS A DAY
AND THE DAY WAS ENDING

And it was standing and it was waiting
And it was a multitude and it looked like an ocean
And it was men and it was women
And it was children and it smelt of leather
And it was cases and it was steam
And it was mouths and it was the word
And it was blank and it was numb
And it was grown-ups and it was coats
And it was dogs and it was whimpering
And it was weeping and it was a train
And it was carriages and it was a ramp
And it was hurrying and it was the shout: inside
And it was pushing and it was hurrying again
And it was rough and it was the tone
And it was hands and it was looks
And it was minutes and it was cramped
And it was no room
And it was almost night and it was a joke
For they were like cattle
And it was a bolt and it was a jolt

And it was moving and it was no air
And it was night and it was time
And it was too long
And it was whispers and it was murmurs
And it was conjectures and it was questions
And it was heat and it was too cramped
And it was weeping again and it was a bucket
And it was four corners and it was a smell
And it was shame
And it was hours and it was hours
And it was hours and it was hours
And it was thirst and it was chaos
And it was falling and it was leaning
And it was a tired prayer
And it was murky water from the ladle

And it was a jolt

And it was listening and it was a hope
And it was a language and it was a country
And it was hours and it was hours
And it was hours and it was hours
And it was forebodings and it was rumours
And it was a fire spreading
And it was snatches and it was words
And it was surely not true

And it was a jolt
And it was true
And it was a strange name

Au-schw-itz

From *Sag doch mal was zur Nacht*

WE WOULDN'T HAVE TAKEN PART

We wouldn't have taken part in this business
We would have held back
Would have stayed at home
With our women, our children, our houses, our hearths
We wouldn't have worn brown or parted our hair or
Worn that unfortunate moustache
We wouldn't have called Sieg and wished Heil
We wouldn't have screamed loudly. We would have gone swing
    dancing

But wait, we did swing dance and boogie woogie
Throwing women over our shoulders
We did shimmy and quickstep
By night we were who we hunted through the streets by day
By night we were the people day saw walk in front of our barrels
By night we were the people food rationing shut out
We were by night the people we would never have let our
    daughters near

We wouldn't have taken part in this business
Till we saw that the minister and the teacher also somehow took
    part
And the lady who let us reach into the sweetie jar
We wouldn't have taken part in this business

I'm telling you
I wouldn't have shoved a toothbrush into anyone's hand and said
Scrub the damn platform, all of it
Wouldn't have said, just one suitcase and you'll get your things
    back after the disinfection
Would never have said faster, faster to the lame old men and
    never you left, your sister right, would never have spat at
    Herr Jakob in the face
But
I wouldn't say that I wouldn't have signed my name, wouldn't
    have scrawled a cross, a yes, in the wrong box at the wrong
    moment

I wouldn't say that I wouldn't have stayed silent once too often
    rather than open my mouth one too many times
I wouldn't say that
I wouldn't have taken part in this business
Somehow
I wouldn't say that I wouldn't have taken part

From *Sag doch mal was zur Nacht*

YOU JUST CAN'T

Call up, leave a voicemail, say something meaningful,
when you're here, standing, smoking in the same room.
Lift children up into the air while their parents are watching,
    practise
by lifting cats into the air as their owners look on,
bait the mini piranhas in the pet shop with broccoli.
Talk about education in Essex, or concrete poetry
with someone who only reads Thomas Mann.
Have curls and straight hair on the same head,
be called Claudia and Paul.
Be grateful for the Autobahn and squash toads flat,
be grateful for the Autobahn and say
you never knew a thing about any Final Solution.

From *Klimaforschung*

LOVERUST

overnight
you have oxidised
next to me

reacted to me
become rusty
you say
golden
I lick your neck
you taste like the
weather vane

From *Klimaforschung*

EXPLANATION

My heart is that ball of wool
Of Ariadne's, wound red through
The labyrinth. If monsters swing along it
Into my web I coil us in,
Spinning, dizzied blind,
I darn them and me
Into a bloody patch,
Sew it all into my breast and call the whole
Thing longing and waiting: formula for love.

From *Klimaforschung*

THIS IS FOR FRIEDERIKE MAYRÖCKER

*Knowledge of a thing prompts love of it. The more
thorough the knowledge, the more searing the love.*

Leonardo da Vinci

I love the thing that you are, are and are like the machine
Bound in a throat the words
Which would like – no – which want what the ears hear
More deeply more searingly love is a cure
A burn a scar hideous on the back of your hand
As it passes your lips like the moon's shadow
The windpipe – its desire for speech – stitched up into
A baggy seam, your forehead pressed against it
To not want to let go, to not be able to stay
In these hours of pale lights in the parlours
Of dressmakers the women who unstitch
Enwearied

From *Klimaforschung*

FOR ANNA

your heart a cuckoo's egg
in your breast of reeds
body against the light
in the X-ray's beam a prism reveals
the foreign matter
no wonder the soul makes ready to fly
wings outstretched
the body heavy
with drowning lungs
and swollen foot, you hardly even
limp anymore, if all the world calls you
daughter of Job, child of Moses
I call you
softly, my eyes closed
machine

From *Klimaforschung*

THE HEART

an artichoke
large as a mango and bruises-blue

can be peeled and exposed
layer for layer

is discerned with astonishment
whether its size

could be home to Eden
between the lungs

was hidden by the rib
from which the apple eater was carved

scarcely any fuss now
about this thing – plantable, sowable

after you fell into my chest's bed

From *Klimaforschung*

RELEASING YOU FROM LIFE

Two or three signatures – | to cancel any binding contracts, then the arrangements, the essentials –

Pack two or three cases | everyone keeps saying these same sentences:

Tell two or three people | a shame, such a life, so soon, so kind, such a kind person

Bury two or three hours | now with their parents, the angels, God watches over

Two or three minutes every year from now | everything, just wait, the Good Lord has an eye, a tooth

Release you from life | for a tooth gnawed you out of the weave of the world

Peel out of the coat | I stand waving, I stand my senses exploding

Throw away your vitamin riches I furrowed within me, within a plastic tub
Vicar says: in all eternity I the watch, the teeth before the cremation, when I say farewell
You out of life: from now on I I mean: such a shame, from now on you out of life

—
— —
—
—
—

From *Klimaforschung*

ARSONIST

you a blaze in me
my heart blisterful
wets my shirt
the fabric ruined
above the heart
there's no going out like this
in public
hair chimneying
in misty rooms
I stand with you
sparks flying

From *Klimaforschung*

\<SHE\>

talks about love
as if it only overcomes others
gnawing at their hands
liquefying their brains
grating their skin
fetching the stars from heaven

\<HE\>

talks about love
like the positioning of an armchair
a fanciful piece of plastering
the engraving on a doorknob
the afternoon downpour around three
the scar on his chin
and the story of how it got there

From *Klimaforschung*

TRAGEDY

Mama always
Warned me

You'll make me betray
The little kid in the cupboard
To the wolf

Papa is sewing
Up an emptied stomach

From *Klimaforschung*

AT HOME

mummyanddaddyandchildandchildssisterandchildsbrotherand
childsuncleandthisisthewaytheladiesrideanddownintheditchand
slobberedbydogandguineapigandhisshortlegsdisappearinto
cracksandyellowbirdincageandnextdoorandnextdoorswifeand
cleanerandcleanershusbandandmummysloveranddaddysblonde
anddaddysblondebeerandmummyspillsanddogdayhotandnext
doorscatandterracedidyll

From *Klimaforschung*

BITCH

took me along
lifted from the box
led by the hand
water from the saucer
placed a collar of cultured pearls around my neck
taught tricks: baking, cooking, sewing on buttons
then one day
abandoned me
after a long drive in a blindfold
or a stick thrown too far

I lifted myself up, discarded my pelt
climbed into high heels and stand now
waiting

From *Klimaforschung*

WHY I DON'T GO THERE?

Well, that's because
I don't feel at home there
Quite queasy
So under pressure
Because everyone's so
And I don't have a fourth
Yet, but soon
Yes, and because the others
Always make such a fuss
A racket about themselves and
These themes
It does sometimes baffle
Me. As a poet you have
No plot and no storyline
And no pretty protagonists
And no arsehole in your lines
And generally in poetry you stand
Howling at the sidelines
And stamp your feet
When the packed-out success bus once again
Soaks you as it drives past
Soaks you with muddy water
And all you can do is howl and stamp
And go home wet
And blame your parents
Doubt in God and above all in yourself and
Your damn cellulite
Because if that weren't
And it were all so
Then long ago
Yes, and someone from one of those agencies
Would have come and would have
And now
Said with a noticeable question mark
And them with such a
Why someone hasn't long ago
Kissed you on the forehead

The whole thing's a load of rubbish
Because it's too warm and suddenly
You can smell the sweat of your publisher
All that oestrogen of the publishing skivvies
Who'd wanted to do something with journalism
And now
The food's expensive too
Hotdog with mustard, no roll, €4.20
Or lemonade or one of those Wall's ice creams
Horrendous, and the few people who recognise you and say
    something
And the people you watch as they try to
Slide over manuscripts
Or in the evening at parties
Business cards of publishing studs
Who just aren't yet aware of
Your cellulite
Somehow I find it unpleasant
I find that it's so removed from my work
From my brooding and hiding away
I'm simply not going
And do have to be careful…
Because the 13th fairy soon sounds like a bitch
But even she had her reasons
If they just forget the invitation…
Arseholes

From *Klimaforschung*

SEX

Stop and go
You up above
To me inside
I yeees
But first and then
Oh, I see
I have some kind of
Man? Contract?
No, condition
In love, engaged
In secret
Oh, I see
What is that
Is that meant to mean?
I can cope with that
I could envelop you
Today after dinner
If you wanted
To give me
A sign
Sun, moon and stars
But these
But those
Are a particular kind
Of exertion
Like our two
Well, when I
Realised what kind
I aroused something
Hot? Cool? Cold?
Veeery old
Understood!
Or rather not!
Together we could
Lift a leg
That is, yours, and then you
Against a wall

Which one? The one in the hall?
Sure. But we can negotiate
Which wall and which leg
Also we need
At least
A fleece, a space, horizon
On which we
Can tabernacle
With your mouth
I could promise myself to me
For each time I said
I – Imemine
As a rule I meant
You – youyouryours
In all seriousness
But the condition!
Yes, it is
Quite ill-considered
By both of us
Worth considering
Count to fifteen
Then the other leg
Now one of yours
Around the other
Of mine but then
And lay your arms down
By your sides
But not without
Enough attention for these zones
Melt, melt everything
Until combined
Fold the newest ingredient
Into the above
We form a dough
Do I have to
Let you rise, let you brew
Or will you bruise?

What exactly are you
And that with me?
I don't seem to know
Anything anymore
And that's before we
Get to the filling
Count to ten
Roll, me, into the blanket
But we
Haven't at all
Rocked
Reeled
Licked each other all over
That's just basic
When was it that
The light was fiddled with?
Did it go out
When the leg
Your one this time
And I here
As always
You say
I
No, just don't say
Anything right now, please
I have to
Concentrate hard
Stop touching
Now
Hands off
No more
All the valuables
Stretched out
In front of me
Just leave it
Just be
Just stay

Just do this
Just act as if
We were through
Cooled down
Harden
As a couple
Come to stand on the top
Of a cake
That's the condition I meant
Count to five
And stop and go

From *Nachrichten aus der Luft*

WOMAN WITH NO LUCK
BETWEEN HER LEGS

Between the halves of her brain
Between the lines
Woman with no ring on her finger
With no in-laws
With no in-laws bending over the tiny bed
With no in-laws bending over the tiny bed and talking to a
    child
With no red lips
With no smooth skin on her hands, her breasts and feet
Woman with no sweetness and no sourness
Woman with no ponytail and no healthy glow and no smell of
    baby
Woman with no dressing gown
Woman with no contract
Woman with no stable job
Woman of a husband with no future
Woman with no husband
Woman with no friend's husband
Woman with no heart; no kidneys, no visa
Woman with no clitoris
Dildo, mood, orgasm
Woman with a desire for peace and quiet
Between the brows, the breasts
Woman with no vision
Woman with no chance of thinner lenses

From *Nachrichten aus der Luft*

PICTURE BOOK UTERUS

How beautifully everything in you is laid out
It compensates for many things
So picturesque, as I can feel
Keeps good shape and is well organ-ised
Such things are inherited; your mother
Must have been very beautiful
(down below)
Here things can grow and hatch
Even nesting will be easy
Precisely here everything is quite
Excellent. Unfolded
I will never look you
In the eyes, Madam

From *Nachrichten aus der Luft*

AND ONE DAY YOU LEAVE
AND TAKE THE DOG

And with the dog all memories
of walks in the park and of petting,
of lying together and those long
Sundays, dogdays where everything had its place,
the leash, the woof and the lick me.
Hopefully he's now got fleas.

From *Nachrichten aus der Luft*

SONG FOR A FOOL

If the stove ring is hot
I'll touch it
If the stove ring is hot
I'll touch it
If the stove ring is hot
I'll touch it
For you

From *Nachrichten aus der Luft*

CHINESE PET

in our wedding photo
the two of us: dragon and phoenix
now you are more panda
and I am your keeper

From *Nachrichten aus der Luft*

I WAS AWFUL

Starting here
Starting today
Starting now
Things will be very different around here
And your head will finally go back
On your neck, so that you can see
Where you have hurt yourself
Remember
How recently
With your head back on your shoulders remember
Me and your wounds
Yes, I was hungry
And yes, I consumed you
So you don't need to remember
Just to forgive
That was me
Without you I am awful
With you I was awful
When nothing has anything to do with you
I am beyond reproach

From *Nachrichten aus der Luft*

I HAVE HURT YOU

To do so I used a spoon
And said many words which I had
Shovelled, cooked, onto my tongue
I used the years against you
Held the knowledge of us hostage
Reminded you that the roses were yellow
Not red
You can reproach me for everything
I have ordered a skip, had the council
Drive it up to the front door. You can throw in
Everything connected with me which you don't want
You say: just one thing will go in here
I'm so tempted to look inside but I hold back
Out of piety
At 4pm they drive the skip away, your heart inside
Quite pale, still swollen with love
And astonishment at how either of us can live
I so gruesome, you so heartless
I'm sorry heals nothing, is only a dogged attack
With a blunt weapon, taken from a basin
Filled with silver for consumption

From *Nachrichten aus der Luft*

THE ENSEMBLE

The greats never returned home
Hamlet, Ophelia, Lear, even Faust and Nathan
And Martha lay under all the others
In the ghetto after liquidisation
In the showers after the gas
So my mother sat, weeping
When the understudies too
Never came back to open the new season

From *Nachrichten aus der Luft*

FORGETTING THE GHOSTS

when I left
I asked them to come with me
I held the door open and lowered my gaze
so that they could move out, become free
in the new home she lived
near the living room window
he in the study near the door
they saw how I slaved away
and their arms lay around my shoulders
without weight or consequence
my thoughts and heart
rose and when I was called away
I shipped everything, packaged and parcelled
my farewells said, and became less at this place
and I forgot to ask them
to come with me into my old life
which they knew so well
it seems to me as if they still live
in the flat which I left
I tell my friend:
forgot my ghosts
and she knows to say
: they won't be long

From *achduje*

TOBY

is toby
did toby
toby fall from air
to earth
yes of course
was toby
all still why
just why
how come
who falls 13th floor
oh goodness di a ter
little sister says no s or l
di a ter, what a di a ter
is what she says
the boy is like
a bbbbb
a bi bi bi
a kind of anima
I understand, says the man from the police
who isn't a policeman but a
psych, p ych
you kn kn know
a bird you mean
yes, little sister no expert
little sister just little sister
so why did toby
you know
what do I know
well certainly your boy
your kid of 13 years
the school says he was good, great, gentle
and and and these unutterables
you know
the boy was 13 and
you know
homo homo the little sister is a source
of wisdom, of under tanding

no, the boy surely wasn't
gay so young, so early
in the school
in the school they say
what are you saying
that another boy
what
that he oved another boy
she says again
just like that normal so normally
for such a small person
little sister
when you're 13 you don't yet love
after all the brain, the heart aren't
yet quite whole
what
well
you know
why is it that we only ever talk around
around
well because
well
so
whatever
what's important is toby
such a disaster
di a ter, yes
when a 13-year-old boy
becomes a bird
everyone else has failed
because they haven't shown by then
what
a ternative
yes, very true
whoever always says that life
is a tragedy, a vale of tears
can hardly wonder

wonder
it almost spells out wound
toby fa en from air
that was a wonder
that was the saddest day
of all sad days
without a ternative
we all
just through this
have
urvived him

From *achduje*

OFTENTIMES

One time the farmer danced so wildly in the mud that the calf
was frightened

One time I took castor oil and lost the child

One time she ran after a man who absolutely didn't want her

One time I wanted to shake an apple from the tree and ten fell
on my head

One time a soldier came and when I went to shake his hand, I
saw that he had none

One time blood rushed to her face when she was meant to
dance a Dashing White Sergeant with the sergeant

One time she peed standing up to warm her feet on the icy
cold field

One time a table of cakes stood there and the whole house
smelt of memories because she wouldn't bake any more

One time he called me by the name of my sister

One time the farmer was so tired he fell asleep on my sister in
the cowshed

One time I told the teacher what happened to us on the farm

One time she came to visit

One time and never again

One time I shook out the duvets and the feathers swirled
through the air like in the fairy tale

One time she said she wanted to visit our brother in town and
the farmer said maybe

One more time he said maybe

One more time she asked

One time I drew a large dog and smudged its outlines
because it is important to remain unpredictable

One time a letter arrived for my sister and the farmer read it
aloud in her room, the farmer read very slowly

One time I held a hand in the darkness, it was warm and soft

One time our mother was here and drank whisky with the
farmer

One time their hands touched as they did so, soon after she
packed her bag and left without waiting for me

One time I came home to an empty house, I had never been
happier

One time a dog fell into the slurry pit
One time the hunter had to come, he too drank whisky
One time my sister said she could run like the wind
One time the window was open before everyone in the house
    was awake, the wind wafted in
One time I stood in my nightdress, it was very early, and I
    gazed after my sister, the way she ran like the wind
One time I placed milk, bread, whisky on the table
One time he touched me, said words I didn't understand,
    showed me secrets
All at once I was and remained my sister, replaced time and
    time again one person with another
One more time I saw the glow worm in the glass, became my
    sister once again
One time my brother then: the wind

                                        From *achduje*

BERLIN SUNBATHER DESCRIBES THE CIRCUMSTANCES

the nightingales – Romeo-bitches, every one –
beat
me up
spread their cloying sweetness over my drums
all it needed was for me to become weak
in this filthy park beneath this ridiculous man
far too young for a young woman
and despite all this incapacitated potency
I became pregnant from the wind and the rain
no one had ever told me how not to
I guess terror had the upper hand
and I had candy floss, a sweetie shop
there between my legs which really
only wanted to carry the girl
safe and sound and home to bed
they too failed, beaten green
and blue by Romeo's bitches
– you only ever hear it (whispered
by people normally), the larks strike
and in this park beating bright day reigns

From *achduje*

SPEAK THE RARE THINGS

Say ocelot
Dodo
Leviathan
Amethyst
Ruby
Caviar
Mink
Unicorn
Xoloitzcuintle
A pure heart
A cheerful mind
Nutmeg
Saffron
Business-class seats

From *achduje*

THREE FLYING MINUTES (EXTRACTS)

Three flying minutes was written as an opera libretto; the opera, with music by Helga Pogatschar, premiered in 2013. The selection here presents four extracts from the libretto.

Hello, is this thing on? Helloooo. Can everyone hear me? And at the very back too? Can you hear me clearly?

This here is the prologue
This is the talk of the aim and the goal
These are the talks of the air and the guilt
These are the talks of Amen and the dirt

The song of Alpha, of Z
The songs of Aleph, of Tet
The songs of age, of merit

This here is the prologue
This here is a soak
This here is a so-called
Entrance

***

You said last Wednesday that you're finding it hard to get up. How did it go for you today? You've been with us for five weeks now. Are you very tired? Describe your daily routine! Do you do sport? Why does that scare you? Could you imagine going on a journey? Describe your situation in your own words…

the black dog
the leaden dress
the feathered night
the creature of fog
the quest made of questions
the questions from leather

the senses' imploring
the many different deceits
the temptation by death
the great silence
the total of time
the body in space
the drug helps
the day dawns
the life: dream

And then I was back. Had climbed out of the bath of lead.

Was back in the texture of the world. My phone rang again,
my vases filled themselves with flowers – or had I simply
stopped seeing them?
They blossomed tiredly before my eyes.
They blossomed for themselves.
They blossomed, blossomed at me and I saw it.

I pack my suitcase.

I pack my suitcase and in it I put a hat.

I pack my suitcase and in it I put a hat and a hat ribbon.

I pack my suitcase and in it I put a hat and a hat ribbon and a
small potted palm.

I pack my suitcase and in it I put a hat and a hat ribbon and a
small potted palm and your promisssssssssssse (keep it!).

***

I pack my suitcase and in it I put a hat and a hat ribbon and a
small potted palm and your promise to join me.

I pack my suitcase and in it I put a hat and a hat ribbon and a
small potted palm and your promise to join me and the

memory of a kiss.

I pack my suitcase and in it I put a hat and a hat ribbon and
a small potted palm and your promise to join me and the
memory of a kiss and the mint lips which kissed it.

I pack my suitcase and in it I put a hat and a hat ribbon and
a small potted palm and your promise to join me and the
memory of a kiss and the mint lips which kissed it and huge
volumes of air in your minutes of silence.

I pack my suitcase and in it I put a hat and a hat ribbon and
a small potted palm and your promise to join me and the
memory of a kiss and the mint lips which kissed it and huge
volumes of air in your minutes of silence and heartbeats.

I pack my suitcase and in it I put a hat and a hat ribbon and
a small potted palm and your promise to join me and the
memory of a kiss and the mint lips which kissed it and huge
volumes of air in your minutes of silence and heartbeats barely
audible down the phone.

I pack my suitcase and in it I put a hat and a hat ribbon and
a small potted palm and your promise to join me and the
memory of a kiss and the mint lips which kissed it and huge
volumes of air in your minutes of silence and heartbeats which
were barely audible down the phone and yet you couldn't
deny that they were there.

I pack my suitcase and in it I put a hat and a hat ribbon and
a small potted palm and your promise to join me and the
memory of a kiss and the mint lips which kissed it and huge
volumes of air in your minutes of silence and heartbeats which
were barely audible down the phone and yet you couldn't
deny that they were there and that they wanted to beat on
your tongue.

I pack my suitcase and in it I put a hat and a hat ribbon and a small potted palm and your promise to join me and the memory of a kiss and the mint lips which kissed it and huge volumes of air in your minutes of silence and heartbeats which were barely audible down the phone and yet you couldn't deny that they were there and that they wanted to beat on your tongue and say to you:

I pack my suitcase and in it I put a hat and a hat ribbon and a small potted palm and your promise to join me and the memory of a kiss and the mint lips which kissed it and huge volumes of air in your minutes of silence and heartbeats which were barely audible down the phone and yet you couldn't deny that they were there and that they wanted to beat on your tongue and say to you and now, now I have to go.

I pack my suitcase and in it I put a hat and a hat ribbon and a small potted palm and your promise to join me and the memory of a kiss and the mint lips which kissed it and huge volumes of air in your minutes of silence and heartbeats which were barely audible down the phone and yet you couldn't deny that they were there and that they wanted to beat on your tongue and say to you and now, now I have to go and pack my suitcase.

So I packed my suitcase and in it I put a hat and a hat ribbon and a small potted palm and your promise to join me and the memory of a kiss and the mint lips which kissed it and huge volumes of air in your minutes of silence and heartbeats which were barely audible down the telephone and yet you couldn't deny that they were there and that they wanted to beat on your tongue and say to you and now, now I have to go and pack my suitcase and tell you that I am waiting and that back then I packed my suitcase with a hat and a hat ribbon and a small potted palm and your promise to join me and the memory of a kiss and the mint lips which kissed it and huge volumes of air in your minutes of silence and heartbeats which were barely audible down the phone and yet you couldn't deny that they were there and that they wanted to beat on your tongue and say to you and now, now I have to go and pack my suitcase and tell you that I will wait and that I really remember everything quite well.

***

but I'll surely die of this

I say to my doctor
who smiles and says, yes, surely
if that's what you want
you could also survive and
live to be 100 and see your grandchildren
marry and your great grandchildren come into the world
but only if you want to
and then she taps the syringe
like they do in films
the syringe between her fingers, up in the air
and a liquid inside and in me a needle
and I choose and get dressed, first
pulling the tube out of my arm
so I stand at the corner and wait for the bus
my children, the grandkids, the weddings, my grandkids'
children, my 100th birthday and right now I am
not 100
but rather simply
here

From achduje

TRANSLATOR'S NOTE

Thanks are due to the many people who provided encouragement, feedback and suggestions throughout the translation process, most particularly to Marisa Rohrbeck, Rebecca DeWald and master of puns Ceris Aston. 'Assumptions about the town' was translated in collaboration with Rebecca DeWald within the framework of Found in Translation.

Thanks of course to Clive Birnie for his vision and trust, and to Nora Gomringer for her faith, encouragement and help in plaiting together the heads of the Hydra.

.

'Banish this gorgeous, finely chiselled linguistic splendou, with its many Hydra-like heads? Tie the heads back into a ponytail so that the text shows just one face?' the author wails. The author is, in this relationship, a crybaby.

Zwischen den Zeilen: Zungen, Nora Gomringer: a speech to the German union of literary translators on the occasion of their 60th anniversary